T0128252

THE
Empowerment
OF LIGHT

G.VONN

authorHOUSE®

AuthorHouse™
1663 Liberty Drive
Bloomington, IN 47403
www.authorhouse.com
Phone: 833-262-8899

Published by AuthorHouse 01/16/2023

ISBN: 978-1-7283-7732-2 (sc)
ISBN: 978-1-7283-7731-5 (e)

Library of Congress Control Number: 2023900633

Print information available on the last page.

CONTENTS

ACKNOWLEDGEMENTS

Thank You
God
Harold*Ta-Tanisha*Faith
Friends*Associates*AuthorHouse
I acknowledge you the reader. May you
continue to journey into spiritual empowerment
by reading the contents of this visionary and
inspirational book. It is comprised of actual
events, affirmations, lessons and meditations. I
do not profess miracles. Rather, enjoyment in
the sanctuary of ancient wisdom is offered. Be
encouraged to rise in consciousness and
behold the true beauty of your inner self. Find
comfort and direction in what your heart and
mind already knows. Observe and honor that:
"Synchronicity Is A Language Of God."

INTRODUCTION

Welcome to "The Empowerment Of Light". This concept defines our relationship with creative living universal energy and manifests itself as daily experiences. You are that light. I am that light. We are that light. So, this poetic message presents life as an intrinsic journey to expand that dynamic power within us. Uniquely designed, this book is intended to provide meaningful paths beyond barriers, programming and illusion as they blend into a tapestry of resonance for individual and collective transformation through: Oneness, Peace, Joy and Love.

Actual visionary experiences flavors the book's contents with a compassionate view of life's dynamics beginning with an initiation. By utilizing lessons, affirmations and meditation, you are encouraged to contemplate and continue your spiritual quest in a sanctuary of inspirational sacred knowledge. Concurrently, it will become apparent that the ultimate goal of this book is to strengthen the connection with: Higher Self - Inner Self - True Self

(All the same)

INITIATION

LEVEL #1

The sun shone in brilliance
While adorning my head
As thoughts of sadness
Embraced my heart instead

I felt completely lost
Causing pain in my soul
I felt deep desire
I longed to be whole

My heart beat fast
As I shielded the fear
I needed real guidance
But I felt relief near

I prayed for the truth
To be it told
I needed renewal
From gloom in my soul

All I truly wanted
Was a world of caring
To be in a life
Of love and sharing

So I focused on freedom
As my deepest goal
Wanting to feel complete
Wanting to be whole

So I forgave the past
Of all that I had done
And I forgave the pain
Caused by everyone

Suddenly it happened
My veil opened wide
Into a knowledge
That was deep deep inside

I beheld the power
Of the masterful flame
Inside the mystic night
From whence life came

LEVEL #2

Desire Opened Up It's Arms
And revealed a blessed sight
It was my higher self
Reaching out beyond the light

The embrace was so majestic
Gleaming with a gentle song
Our energies caressed each other
Because we knew we belong

The energy was very loving
The energy had a golden flight
Glowing with deep wisdom
With projections of delight

It was such a miracle
A wonderful dream come true
Our minds and hearts were in harmony
We sang I feel so close to you

We vibrated as we were one
Our thoughts created a single flow
Our visions reached out to each other
While our enchantment was all aglow

Knowing love and infinity are one
We soared through the sea of life
Knowing that real happiness exists
When kindred spirits unite

Life sprang as revelation
Like a cosmic mystical dance
And love became divine
Like a deep spiritual romance

We were grateful for the journey
Of universal ascensions to God
Imploding and exploding
Life's pendulum swinging rod

We pulsated with awareness
Internalized the truth we found
And externalized a sweet rapture
And life became unbound

We felt real purpose
In the living and loving sea
We felt we are one
And inside we are free

It was fulfillment
To flow in the now
Inside the oasis
Where all essence is thou

The power was so strong
Cascading from the night
As we both experienced
The hidden lessons of light

We learned we are masters
Rising all are we
Manifesting one power
All from one tree

We had journeyed beyond illusion
With the horizon all so near
Letting loneliness loose meaning
Releasing sorrow anger and fear

We floated beyond commands
Beyond rose colored walls
Feeling the warmth of release
We entered freedom halls

We understood that in others
Are our experiences we see
We said I see the light in you
It also shines in me

We knew to do unto others
Allows the mirror to reveal
Images we perceive as self
As ways for the soul to heal

Inside each other
We let programming sail away
As knowledge became so vibrant
In each manifested day

LEVEL #3

We glowed and radiated
A universal conscious sun
Because we are creative power
And inside we are all one

We were flying with the angels
We were flying up high
We sang with our friends
And danced through the sky

We were as before
Inside a love so deep
Like a lingering memory
That we felt in our sleep

It was so very wonderful
To return to the glow
Wrapped in faith and truth
And freedom we longed for so

From transparency we came
And gloriously we had returned
Knowing the divine hidden truth
Of oneness that we yearned

Sacredness was shinning in us
We felt it's presence whole
We learned about empowerment
As we merged soul to soul

One spirit was merged and flowed
Displaying cosmic might
One mind reflected and knew
The lessons of the light

Our heart radiated and healed
Divine knowledge of the one
Our body evolved and felt
In God thy will be done

There was celebrated transformation
With triumph over pain
There was empowerment in oneness
In light we did proclaim

Laws of Light

#1
As I Look At Others
Into Self I Do See
Because The Light In You
Is Also Light In Me

#2
As I Do To Others
To Self I Also Do
And What I Do To Me
I Also Do To You

The Four Paths

#1

Oneness

EVENT

The air felt thick and vibrated with strong intention while infinite reality embraced my soul. My grandfather was not home but grandmother and I envisioned his voice echoing throughout the house. This woman who fed the hungry in her home every week and consoled the downhearted heard his voice. I heard his voice. He was calling for help and struggling in imminent danger. Empathically, my grandmother responded with prayer and assurance that he would be ok. Hours later, he returned home wet and exhausted after being rescued from a capsized fishing boat. Our prayers were answered. We were all thankful for our positive thought and connection with the oneness of God.

AFFIRMATION

The Power Of Oneness
Is My Energy
I Am Oneness
And Oneness Is Me

LESSONS

1.1
BREATH

Welcome to the crystal gates
The entrance to power unbound
Focus on the breath
Beyond the matrix sound

Inhale and exhale
For oneness to reveal
Let breathing be the focus
To center and to heal

The breath in meditation
Is life that we receive
It's a deep internal passage
Into that which we perceive

Our breath is our guidepost
As vibration instructs the soul
That each and every experience
From attention does behold

1.2
ATTENTION

Life seems so serene
Like melodies from afar
As we project our attention
Into our own inner star

Then melodies start to evolve
And morph from the past
As we yearn for guidance
From attention that we cast

We sway in one vibration
In an exotic flowing dance
And with our attention
We enter a deep deep trance

We touch kiss and embrace
The attention we did part
Bridging our perception
Exchanging one beating heart

1.3
PERCEPTION

Heart embraces heart
To heal and hold on tight
So we project the reality
Within our realm of sight

Perception seeks the truth
Just like butterflies
Soaring from cocoons
To rainbow colored skies

Because like butterflies
We transmit passionate thought
Into the perceptions
Of what our hearts have sought

It's energy of one heart
It's energy of one mind
That engages perception
And visions of humankind

1.4

VISION

As energy vibrates into matter
Within eternal infinite light
It flows from desire
To the vision that's in sight

Visions seek themselves
And are constantly aware
That like attracts like
This internal law we share

Co-creators of one vision
Heed the cosmic voice
We're in a school as students
We're seekers all by choice

We emulate our rainbows
With one melodious array
Ascending through our visions
Into goals day by day

1.5
GOALS

We yearn for the truth
Inhabited deep within
From ancestral hearts
From goals kin to kin

We climb beyond the walls
To reveal the goal of one
We survive initiations
That unveil our inner sun

Because the master inside
Transcends individual goals
Rising beyond the programs
Of self seeking souls

For now is the moment
Where goals rise from the night
Learning through challenges
Oneness glowing and in flight

#2

Peace

EVENT

One night I had an extraordinary dream. I beheld a magical garden arrayed with vivid flowers in an embrace of twilight existence. Everything was alive. I could hear nature's heartbeat pulsating creation. The next night, I fainted trying to call my parents while envisioning my spirit floating to the ceiling into a massive grey cloud of infinity. My friends called 911 and I was immediately transported to emergency surgery for a severely ruptured appendix. It was doubtful that I would survive. However, a loving angel had telepathically informed me "There is much more for you to do." From that day, I continue to find comfort knowing the relevance of peace.

AFFIRMATION

The Power Of Peace
Is My Energy
I Am Peace
And Peace Is Me

LESSONS

2.1
IDENTITY

When God is our attraction
And that with which is adorned
Identity paves a path
As each new day is born

Identity has the power
Within the collective vow
To reflect the peaceful self
That all embrace as Thou

Raising this frequency
Opens the identity seal
It causes us to acknowledge
That living light is for real

And moment by moment
Beyond our intellects
We know our true identity
Seeks nature and reflects

2.2
NATURE

We ride the omnipresence
Inside we do glow
Knowing we're the masters
In all of nature's flow

We acknowledge our nature
In reverence everyday
Our journey seeks omniscience
In all we do and say

Nature reveals omnipotence
It is from whence we first came
It's peace is shining and rising
It's magnificence will be our gain

So as we connect with nature
Unto it we need to be true
Because we are it's mirrors
Transforming grace anew

2.3
GRACE

Yeah we faithfully walk
Through the valley so wide
We feel true grace in us
That is deep peace inside

We walk through the garden
With initiations on how to live
Climbing over the mountain home
In reverent grace we give

Our hearts are wide open
As our minds humbly say
The grace in our souls
Uplifts us every day

We do feel God's touch
We do feel God's embrace
In us In us
We attract God's true grace

2.4
ATTRACTION

Let the eternal shine in us
And sing of peace inside
Let us attract true brilliance
So we will shine and glide

In our flames of attraction
Vibration embraces hearts
Dancing in a chorus
We sing to never part

We attract as we dance
As spirits we do sow
And reap seeds of Heaven
Within our ecstatic glow

Enlightenment is reaped
Attraction reunites as one
Within our committed alliance
To service our reflecting sun

2.5
SERVICE

Walk in a determined heartbeat
Service should never cease
Treat others with fairness
For benevolence to increase

Be in the creator's image
Acknowledge the feeling well
It's all about the service
It's our emancipation bell

Then we can rightfully proclaim
God's service walks through me
We've discovered an ancient law
We've discovered a wondrous key

So we rise all together
Divine service is a noble flow
We connect with each other
In peace we are aglow

#3

Joy

EVENT

While flying home from my father's funeral, I could "smell" smoke in the plane. Then I "saw" smoke in the plane. Immediately, gas masks dropped as the smoke intensified into a thick cloud. We held hands, silently prayed and contemplated our lives. In remembrance of dad's mentoring vibration and expanding wisdom, I repeatedly reaffirmed mentally "I Trust You God", "I Trust You God". "I Trust You God". The plane made an emergency landing and we were safely bused to a terminal gate. While waiting for another plane, someone said "Maybe we are in Heaven". I contemplated a "Heavenly State of Mind". Our journeys were blessed and protected. We were safe and joyful to be alive.

AFFIRMATION

The Power Of Joy
Is My Energy
I Am Joy
And Joy Is Me

LESSONS

3.1
JOURNEY

Creation is evolving
As we gently walk the vine
Journeying into the joy
Of one infinite mind

Knowing no birth or death
Just a coming and going soul
We journey in each temple
To observe and behold

Expanding each seeking body
We journey through the night
We learn and reflect
In silence shining bright

Knowing we're in training
Devoted so bright and pure
We journey in this universe
Through wisdom we endure

3.2
WISDOM

Our bodies are joyful temples
Amidst the gentle flow
Celebrating wisdom within
That's beyond what we know

And because collective wisdom
Addresses itself as I
We know we are just one self
Learning how to fly

Our light magnifies within
Gleaming and glowing bright
And we resonate in wisdom
As sparkles in the night

And beyond all the boundaries
There's wisdom in each soul
Raising our frequency
In freedom to have and hold

G.VONN

3.3

FREEDOM

Riding the freedom boat
Will dissolve all the pain
As we escape the cage
For longing not to remain

And with all the strange things
We do in the cage of life
All we need to do is awaken
To be free from stress and strife

With each joyful event
In spirit hand and hand
Freedom becomes real
Displaying where we stand

Freedom surpasses programming
As we learn meaningful things
That we are more than a body
And our faith has giant wings

3.4
FAITH

Our faith is inside of us
As we learn each new song
Our relief is inside of us
We're here and we belong

When we praise with joy
And awareness that is true
It leads and heeds us on
To manifests all anew

Because with each thing we do
We contribute to the whole
And we know that with faith
Our lives begin to unfold

So let us all have faith
Embrace it with mind and heart
Open up God's gates
Behold the inner star

3.5

GATEKEEPERS

It is true It is true
Gatekeepers are gloriously wide
Just look in the infinite mirror
As we rise side by side

What we continue to envision
Are gatekeepers of deep caring
We seek fields of compassion
And understanding and sharing

Because gatekeepers are us
Mastering our every call
We are opening up the lock
And knocking down the wall

We are the gatekeepers
Of serene illuminated rays
We know the inner secret
Is to glow in joyful days

#4

Love

EVENT

When mom could speak, she had called for her husband and mother. Now silent and still, I could envision her spirit elevating above her physical body. It looked like a light of deep compassion rising into a field of ultimate tranquility. This glowing living light suspended beyond time and space and transformed into a cosmic melody of a slow vibrational dance. Her soul was transitioning into a glorious existence and my heart respectfully honored the revelation of her true self. Her beautiful soul was transcending in glory and destined to the arms of God. The portal was closed as she returned home after devotedly serving God in an ongoing wave of devotion, faith and deep compassionate love.

AFFIRMATION

The Power Of Love
Is My Energy
I Am Love
And Love Is Me

LESSONS

4.1
SACREDNESS

Space and time are infinite
We soar through the flow of life
We dance in sacredness
When consciousness does unite

And pulsating in the flow
Love becomes all we find
We ascend in sacredness
With spirit heart and mind

Sacred spirit keep shining in us
Empower our presence whole
As we learn reciprocity
And you gently lift each soul

Let spirits shine and flow
From the cosmic night
Let minds reflect and behold
The blessings of the light

4.2
BLESSINGS

Let our hearts feel the strength
And blessings from the one
Let our bodies evolve and heal
In God thy will be done

For loving is all there is
This is the only way
We are rising in our blessings
Each and every day

And in this revelation
Blessings are evermore
Moving and morphing
Through the crystal door

The victorious ones are us
With rays of blessed thought
The journey is connected
Circling to the home we sought

4.3

HOME

As masterful essence
We embrace life in all we do
Home is inside of me
And also inside of you

And when we use life lessons
To reveal our home as one
Instantly we understand
All that we have done

Home home
Into transparent light
Life is so spectacular
And all is God and right

Engrained to this day
The comfort of this place
Home is woven in love
In the comfort we embrace

4.4

BEAUTY

We are becoming beautiful
Evolving with endless care
We've moved beyond the veil
Of illusion into prayer

We continue to evolve
As beautiful stars that love
Inside our multi-worlds
Everywhere and above

Spiritual beauty is us
With rainbows wide and far
In our collective action
We each become a star

Within our beautiful rainbows
We are reaching a higher goal
We are embracing the power
As love completes the whole

4.5
POWER

We sustain a release within
As all appearances are gone
Life shares universal power
That's here and far beyond

Life is abundant energy
That flows from deep inside
Power flows in synchronicity
As we manifest and we glide

And as this transformation
Reflects the path we trod
We share majestic power
From an infinite eternal God

For ultimate is this love
That of which we hold
Power is inside all of us
A universal living soul

Meditation #1

The Power Of Light
Is My Energy
I Am Light
And Light Is Me

The Power Of Oneness
Is My Energy
I Am Oneness
And Oneness Is Me

The Power Of Peace
Is My Energy
I Am Peace
And Peace Is Me

The Power Of Joy
Is My Energy
I Am Joy
And Joy Is Me

The Power Of Love
Is My Energy
I Am Love
And Love Is Me

The Power Of Light
Is My Energy
I Am Light
And Light Is Me

Meditation # 2

We Are Rising In Light
Empowered All Are We
We Know And Feel The Light
Of Divine Energy

We Are Rising In Oneness
Empowered All Are We
We Know And Feel The Oneness
Of Divine Energy

We Are Rising In Peace
Empowered All Are We
We Know And Feel The Peace
Of Divine Energy

We Are Rising In Joy
Empowered All Are We
We Know And Feel The Joy
Of Divine Energy

We Are Rising In Love
Empowered All Are We
We Know And Feel The Love
Of Divine Energy

We Are Rising Light
Empowered All Are We
We Know And Feel The Light
Of Divine Energy

BIBLIOGRAPHY

Now retired, the author's primary professional experiences include: administration; quality improvement; community outreach; multicultural outreach; mental health; intergenerational programming and teaching. She is a Peacemaking Circle Facilitator and Reiki Master Teacher. God, her B.A. in Psychology and life-long interest in indigenous spiritual practices have impacted the contents of this book. In addition, experiences through mutual relationships and care-giving experiences have provided impetus to her sharing this book that promotes the spiritual-empowerment of higher consciousness. She is quoted in another book saying: "We are all learning that the oneness we all share is love. There is nothing else."

Printed in the United States
by Baker & Taylor Publisher Services